swoop

SWOOP

Poems

HAILEY LEITHAUSER

Graywolf Press

This publication is made possible, in part, by the voters of Minnesota through a Minnesota State Arts Board Operating Support grant, thanks to a legislative appropriation from the arts and cultural heritage fund, and through grants from the National Endowment for the Arts and the Wells Fargo Foundation Minnesota. Significant support has also been provided by Target, the McKnight Foundation, Amazon.com, and other generous contributions from foundations, corporations, and individuals. To these organizations and individuals we offer our heartfelt thanks.

Winner of the 2012 Emily Dickinson First Book Award established by the Poetry Foundation to recognize an American poet over the age of forty who has yet to publish a first book.

Published by Graywolf Press
250 Third Avenue North, Suite 600
Minneapolis, Minnesota 55401

www.graywolfpress.org

Published in the United States of America

ISBN 978-1-55597-657-6

2 4 6 8 9 7 5 3 1
First Graywolf Printing, 2013

Library of Congress Control Number: 2013939551

Cover design: Jeenee Lee Design

Cover art: Paul Klee (1879–1940) © 2013 Artists Rights Society (ARS), New York. Blumenmythos (Flower Myth). 1918. Watercolor on chalk ground on tissue on newspaper on cardboard, 20.0 x 15.8 cm. Inv. Smlg. Sprengel I, 112. Photo: Michael Herling / Aline Gwose. Sprengel Museum, Hannover, Germany. Image copyright © The Metropolitan Museum of Art. Image source: Art Resource, NY.

Acknowledgments

Grateful acknowledgment is made to the following journals and anthologies in which these poems, some in earlier versions, first appeared:

Agni Online: "Sex Circumspect," "Crowbar, " "Sex Odalisque," "Brass Knuckles"

The Antioch Review: "Inspiration," *"Mono No Aware"*

The Cincinnati Review: "Schadenfreude," "O Sorrow, O Bother"

Connotation Press: An Online Artifact: "Judder," "Katzenjammer," "Illaqueable," "Zho," "Memoirs," "Rhyparographer," "Nellipot," "Whither the Lamplight," "Famulus," "Hophound," "Venusaphobia"

The Gettysburg Review: "Sex Alfresco," "I Love Me, Vol. I," "I Recant, Vol. II," "Apologia," "Loneliness," "Boys of L.A.," "Zen Heaven"

Innisfree: "Shoot-Out at the So-So Corral," "Rapture," "Sex Fiasco," "Sex Obstreperous"

The Iowa Review: "Paean: Moon"

The Journal: "Romance"

Meridian: "Scythe," "Dolor," "Guillotine"

Pleiades: "The Old Woman Gets Drunk with the Moon"

Poetry: "Was You Ever Bit by a Dead Bee?" "*O,* She Says," "Delirium," "Fever," "Frostbite," "Bad Sheep," "Mockingbird"

Poetry Daily: "Inspiration," "Sex Rubenesque," "Pip, Mid-Sea"

River Styx: "Sex Rubenesque"

TriQuarterly Online: "Charm against Insomnia," "Rescue"
Stoneboat: "Jiminy"
Subtropics: "Veritas Interruptus"
Unsplendid: "We Few Born beneath a Bitter Star," "The Voluminous Diva"
Virginia Quarterly Review: "Metrophobia," "Cuniculous," "Tragematopolist"

"Having Discovered a Windfall by the Side of the Road, the Cautious Miser Is Visited by the Angel of Profligacy" appeared in the anthology *IOU: New Writing on Money*, published by Concord Free Press.

"The Old Woman Gets Drunk with the Moon" appeared in *The Best American Poetry 2010*.

"I Recant, Vol. II." appeared in *The Crafty Poet*, published by Wind Press.

"Pip, Mid-Sea" was printed as a limited-edition broadside at the Virginia Arts of the Book Center, Charlottesville, Virginia.

Many, many thank yous to the friends and family members without whose help this book would not have been possible, to brother David who sent me the first palindrome that got the book going, to Charles Leithauser and Joan Hope, James Arthur, Sandra Beasley, Karl Elder, Jason Gray, Diana B. Kuhl, Greg McBride, and Kevin McFadden.

Also my deepest gratitude to the Maryland State Arts Council for their generous grant, to Jeff Shotts and the good people of Graywolf, and the members of the Poetry Foundation.

This book is dedicated to the memory of D. Melba Leithauser

Contents

swoop

Scythe

If it could speak it would offer
you excess; it would

offer you *more*.
It would offer you sleep

without dream
in its keep in the field,

in its shed where the moon
lifts her slim drowsy

sword.
It would gossip of stars;

it would cultivate myths
of the muscular tendrils

and vine
of your neck.

It would say what it wants,
and it wants it non-

stop,
is result,

a world that's the same
at the start

as the end,
that it wants like a river

wants flood and a fire
wants hunger,

two bottomless,
unchanging pockets,

the one
that is larder, the other

one locust.

Was You Ever Bit by a Dead Bee?

I was, I was—by its posthumous chomp,
by its bad dab of venom, its joy-buzzer buzz.
If you're ever shanked like the chump
that I was, by the posthumous chomp
of an expired wire, you'll bellow out prompt
at the pitiless shiv when it does what it does.
Was *you?* I was. By its posthumous chomp,
by its bad dab of venom, its joy-buzzer buzz.

Schadenfreude

So often ironic,
at times caustic, despotic,

and always so
honestly,

profoundly
Teutonic,

that the mere sight
of the word

stirs a not quite
contrite,

slight
crimp of the lip.

How simple the way
that it plays to our need

to see someone
not us,

caught in the thrall
of a just,

karmic
pratfall,

to snigger the gloom
of the other

guy's grand, moody
doom.

It's basic:

She saddens, he gladdens.
He rises, she flops.

Diverting enough
to name a rare

tonic, or exotic
parfum for it, sell it in fat-

bottomed bottles
shaped like a tear,

an attar
of pleasure, a tincture

of voyeur,
dabbed coyly,

adroitly,
at the back of the ear.

Sex Alfresco

Never one-volt love, nor even
    lightning bolt's severe and clearer candle;
  nor tact of mooncalf's cautious pawing
    with feathered chaise and bed to cleave in;
nor ease of maid and master's backstair scandal,
    its closeting of coddled mauling,

but ever brisk, and bare, and rarely softened,
  a shrouding bower finds us nabbed and handled;
    in an ample, moony bramble, briar-bitten;
at a doorway, pinned and hidden; behind a shading stable,
    leather-sored, and lather-ridden.

Extreme Season

Delirium

Such green, such green,
this apple, tea and celadon,

this emerald and pine and lime
unsheathed to make

a miser weep, to make his puny
bunions shrink; these seas

and seas of peony, these showy
tons of rose

to urge a musted monk disrobe,
a lamaseried nun unfold;

such breathy, breathy moth
and wasp, such gleeful,

greedy bee to bid
the bully hearts of cops

and bosses sob,
to tell a stubby root unstub, a rusted

hinge unrust, the slug unsalt,
to stir the fusted

lungs to brim, the skin to sting,
the dormant,

tinning tongue to singe and hymn.

FEVER

The heat so peaked tonight
the moon can't cool

a scum-mucked swimming
pool, or breeze

emerge to lift the frowsy
ruff of owls too hot

to hoot (the mouse and brown
barn rat astute

enough to know to drop
and dash), while

on the bunched up,
corkscrewed sheets of cots

and slumped brass beds,
the fitful twist

and kink and plead to dream
a dream of air

as bitter cruel as winter
gale that scrapes and blows

and gusts the grate
to luff

the whitened ashes from the coal.

Dolor

How elegant and weird as
daggers, this shadow-

lingered door, the ragged field,
the creak and swell

and settling beneath
the pantry boards, this scattershot

of crow and jay, the harried
burrowing of voles,

the crop's collapse; what
withering, what excess

scrap, the gourd,
the vine, the rust of brittle

color spasm saps,
and then the blackened ice,

the dusk-dim walk on boot-
rung path, the dark

and covert earth,
the moon a great and yellow

clock, the warren, pen,
the cellar, shed and north-faced porch,

the sere and barren garden locked.

FROSTBITE

Less a nip than gnaw,
the way a goat,

tethered, will ruminate
a rope; the way

each *in extremis* tip
of ear and nose

unbuds, or snail-
like toe, curled

dreamily, lets
go too fat a foot,

cinching filament
and tendril, pinch

by stony pinch
until the pulse exhausts

and flickers down
to drowse and numb,

the sleep so close,
so old,

so mild inside the placid
scald

and hissing of the snow.

Jiminy

Dear small, pleasant time machine,
dear harbinger of blankets and socks,
you who are led by the hand by darkness
into the darkness of cellar and hearth.
Dear intimate tenant of pantries,
one-man chorus of soup bones and roots,
in what great labyrinth or garden,
what Zion of drainage and damp cement
did you calibrate first so dutiful an elegy,
so sad a SOS?

Shoot-Out at the So-So Corral

It is possible
someone
is coming for you.

It is possible someone
is gunning for you.
There is a general

feeling that General
MacArthur, or
his partners in blue,

are coming for someone
who is now,
or is not now, you.

My God, says the firing squad,
how we all
have our ups and our downs.

My God, sings the swung
cattle prod,
how we all have our downs

and our ups.
The moral:
Aim your steps

to the left,
your sights to the right,
or,

in other words:

Keep your guns
snug
at your thigh, your eyes

on the trophy
or tiger or skies,
your wit,

and your powder,
dryer
than dustbowls

of mountain ground,
shanty town,
yellow corn flour.

Charm against Insomnia

Little mouse, little
gray hunger
that nibbles
the night to a bony
toothpick,
little possibility
of impossible things,
glimmer of nothing
like hope,
little shadow
that dreams,
small genius of bad teeth
and ice,
angel of wire,
of colic, of palsy-
thin kittens,
contain like a penny
or aspirin,
your acids and bitters;
cart off on your coattails
those vulture-rich
contrails, your spidery
roses or doses
of splinters.
Bugger and sod off,
blister and suffer,
wither, fester, lackluster,
besnuff, beshrivel,
becroak, benight,
belabor, bellbind, be gone!

Rapture

Such
terrific
stuff, akin
in compass
to an ocean's greatest
rise or
deepest,
muffled dungeon,
or sometimes to a sweep
of summer's
sudden wind
with all the cupboard's
cups and plates and loose
door chatter toyed
with, joining
in,
but always like some broken,
glad, glad bells, or
famished ravage
of a burst
groundswell, it
pours
its weeping joy,
its gallon-pounds of
blood and bust as if
into a tub
or drum, but instead into a fleshy
thimble
jerky as a rum red
jig, and frangible
as violins or
fine bird rib.

Guillotine

If it could speak it would say
tickle, tickle,

s'il vous plait.
Or maybe, *redder, redder,*

or maybe *no,*
never, yes—whichever

word is the one
word it thinks best.

If it could tease,
it wouldn't;

if it would pause for an honorable
cause, it couldn't.

It has a cousin,
distant,

it calls *chaise*
electrique;

it has siblings
called *bomb* and called

hello, so long,
and it once had an auntie

named *cement overcoat,*
till she learned

how to float.
It hopes when no longer

of purpose
or use to the state

to reincarnate;
it yearns

with a yearning that smolders,
to return

as a ladder
leading more or less

somewhere,
a scissor, a razor, a sickle

dropped
in high grass,

quick as a pin,
lost as a nickel,

that insistently
whispers

fickle, and *fickle.*

Sex Fiasco

No use sighing over slipped discs,
she says, and what better bitter could there be
      than she to be beyond and above,
  to suffer slightly, hover faintly, over this
grand thud, this fluttered pink and colored rosy
      dead weight of love.

  What greater nadir for a weighty hip's
mis-grip, what apter riff or eulogy for turgid knees
      and wilted, butter-fingered flips,
what wryer shove, less lilted quip. Says she:
    There's no use crying over spilt lips.

From the Grandiloquent Dictionary

Judder

When junk gives a shudder, like a tractor
more quaint than intact, like lapsed reactors,
pipes worn and contorted, a Toyota
that's done for, or outdated aorta.

Katzenjammer

Think of the yowl of three senile felines.
Think of a buzz saw's black, sauerkraut whine.
Imagine ten screeched, unleashed violins.
Imagine the dawn that follows the gin.

Metrophobia

I, too dislike it, or at least I find
too much of it bromidic and unrhymed,
muffled in a fog of cottony prose,
frightened of shadows or stepping on toes.

Inspiration

Some flim-flam grand slam, glitchy
as religion, this is, with its chronic

key-and-padlock, hit-and-missy cerebellum,
its sturm and drangish, bum-

rushed, all-thumbed cockalorum. How near,
to use the fizzle of yet another

wet-squibbed metaphor, the tepid fever spike
of a heart-junked hypochondriac

frothing for a blunted, lovestruck glint of moon,
or in a bare austerity squiring a siren

star, rats and blinder moles gathered in a dampish,
lamp-black burrow can,

tittering and stirred like weirder
choirs, rise up mindful and consider fire.

O, She Says

O, she says (because she loves to say *O*),
O to this cloud-break that ravels the night,
O to this moon, its mouthful of sorrow,
O shallow grass and the nettle burr's bite,

O to heart's flare, its wobbly satellite,
O step after step in stumbling tempo,
O owl in oak, *O* rout of black bat flight,
(*O* moaned in Attic and Esperanto)

O covetous tongue, *O* fat fandango,
O gnat tango in the hot, ochered light,
O wind whirred leaves in subtle inferno,
O flexing of sea, *O* stars bolted tight,

O ludicrous swoon, *O* blind hindsight,
O torching of bridges and blood boiled white,
O sparrow, and arrow, and hell below,
O, she says, because she loves to say *O*.

Paean: Moon

O sob, O butter-colored breast,
not a tub but a ton of this
mellifluous, unscented lust—

this clambering, untended mist,
coagulate and rubbed and glassed.
O sob for butter-colored breasts,

exhausted shutter clatter, rust
of lumbering and silly bliss,
unscented, mellifluous. Lust

was never better gladdened dust
than inkling's nod, than reminisce
of buttered O and sob, this breast

of nuzzled frost, of puddled feast.
Beneath, a sea surpassed, embossed
with scent mellifluous, and lust

that's dropped from cached, posh, brass, lost host,
vast piccolo, fresh blunderbuss:
O butter sob, O color, breast,
mellifluous, unscented lust.

We Few Born beneath a Bitter Star

Considering stars, you consider disaster,
a heart's slapstick hiccup, a Mongolian flea,
the axeman's fat thumb, and ho-hum that comes after.
But consider what stars consider disaster—
the gluons and muons and gamma-ray blasters
that ass-whup into dross those milksops who believe
that stars they consider, consider disaster
a heart's slapstick hiccup, a Mongolian flea.

Romance

Like I care.
Like I'm scared,
like I'm quaking
in my flip flops
about spring
shaking
its ta-tas,
its neonate, bulbiform tabula
rasas;
like I'm induced
to declare
by a mendicant
heart, a hobo—ha!—
its vena
and cava,
its blood blasting tuba—
some sort of surrender,
a red rover,
red rover
send-the-stupidly-
roscid-
pellucid-
girl-over;
like
I'm a kind to beware
undying
others or somethings,
as if somewhere
there's change that is spare
and its shining
the shimmer-
less toss
of my hair;

like I'm eager to moss,
like
I'm hell bent on
spawning
a moon;
like
I'm dying to dare
the ampere;
like I'm beating
the skin
of a drum:
come here,
here, here,
come.

Sex Circumspect

From under dashboards, behind swing doors,
    dusting dirt from a silk-lined skirt, she emerges
  lipstick freshed, her modest bust immaculately
buttoned up. O never was there vestal more demure
    than ardent, pleasing she who urges
  carnal lures with such schemed subtlety

    to keep a peek discreet; all l'amours toujours
kept under wraps and off the books, purged
      of leak or rumor, assiduously free
of exposé; the only tease or oo-la-la to be observed,
      one nylon run below the knee.

In Praise of Flattery

Syrupy,
purplish,
undulant
prose,
O
enter me
here;
pour more
and more
sugar into
my titillated,
palliated,
prostitute ear.
Drench and
immerse
my unsweetened
ego,
slather with honey
my vinegary
psyche.
Validate my
external
eternally,
and douse
the internal
with similar
treacle
to urge me
dive deep
and drown
in word nectar.

I Love Me, Vol. I

How nobler than a Toblerone am I.
How fit, well-equipped for jury duty,
for taking on grand dames and the snooty
perky-hootered (so loftily and high
rise mine own to sky). How plum-or-peachly
amply-seated, how golder-haired, am I,
vibrissae of Birman or Somali,
articulatio genus of a bee.
But when some wooer comes to coo, what kind
of aetherish, unblemished dish would plumb
this fleshed Elysium? What hymn be hummed
to me, which paradigm be not struck blind;
how find that nonpareil prepared to score
this vessel of unbested metaphor?

I Recant, Vol. II

I'm not a silkworm. I'm not a walnut
soaked in wine, not an almond in Cointreau.
I am not thought vast within a pillow,
not a labyrinth, not cryptic inkblot.
I have not roused an old souse from her rut,
have not started a riot in Cairo,
have stirred no deep, deliquescent sorrow.
I have caused no argument in Zagat.
I am unaddressed in the best cafes
where I am lesser thumb, a background cough,
underpaid, scant hoodoo, verminous fluff.
Among proffered options I am unweighed,
in mulitiple choice, when compared to you,
oozy rat in a sanitary zoo.

Bad Sheep

Midnight's merely blue,
but me, me, me, I'm
through
and through
sloe, cracked soot-
on-a-boot,
nicotine spat, licorice whip.
You can scratch, scratch, scratch
but I stay underskin true
to ebony, ink, crowberry, pitch;
hoist me up by my hooves
and shake till I'm shook, I'm still
chock full of coke, fuliginous
murk.
O there's swart in my soul,
coal by the bag,
cinders and slag,
scoriac grit, so please
come, comb
through my fleece with hands pallid
as snow and watch
how they grow tarry, raven,
stygian, ashed—
or, if you wish, clean me with bleach
I won't
flinch, just char
down to a core of caliginous
marrow,
pure carbon, atramentous,
utterly piceous,
shadowed, and starless,

each clumpity clump
and eclipse of my heart raptly
reburnishing
a woolgather dark.

Crowbar

If it could speak it would say,
Clean

up in aisle three;
would shower

the day with debris
of off-key *mea*

culpas.
It fancies itself

the lost doppelganger
of a mid-

fifth-century saber,
practicing its rattle

when not at the table.
It's prone to chip

stoneware and fracture
decanters, to trampling a mirror

or rim of rare crystal,
and it ponders

and ponders
with thoughts

bordering
wonder, the odd snag

of an ankle or dactyl,
the brave punch

bowl bulge at the back
of the skull,

aesthetic
bendings in a mandible

and clavicle,
porcelain swell

of a tea-cup patella.

Sex Obstreperous

O Naomi did I moan a moan
too odious; did I rasp a ruined gasp too proud?
Was my sweetest lying unenticing
and my crooning just palaver chattered to a drone,
my pillow talk an awkward spout,
my coos, a black crow crying?

Did I couch a murmur overriding and untuned,
growl an innuendo too aroused?
Were my sighings those of mufflers dying;
did I snore like a platoon? Did I pout or crowd or groan,
O dear, revered Naomi, was I loud?

Apologia

So sorry for the mundane dance,
and even more the poor romance,
the pond-dropped glove, the might-have-been
that lingers like a splinter's pain.

So sorry for the drab advance,
so sorry for the bungled dance—
the stoned faux pas, the lipstick stain,
the souring of flat champagne,

the third, and fourth, and tenth offense,
and through it all to still remain
so sorry for the wretched dance
with all its gaffes and botched campaigns,

the timorous and smutty glance,
this fool gut-tug, again, again,
its tedium of worn refrain:
So sorry, sorry for the dance.

From the Grandiloquent Dictionary

Illaqueable

These ten animals I slam in a net:
a flat-foot, knock-kneed flock of fat egrets,
a damp lamb, dumb ram, a wing-withered drake,
a limp, listless slither of tongue-tied snakes.

Zho

Is this cattle or yak? Or sly, hybrid
zooid that's stacking the deck? Not the kid
of a goat, not a male *lama glama,*
not even its own cud-chomping mama.

Cuniculous

One? No, a dozen, half-cousined conies,
a trip of lapins, covey of bunnies,
a husk of hares, a snare, a bagged cavort,
a wrack, a crammed sack of snagged lagomorphs.

Veritas Interruptus

She said:

"What
the unstoppered
id did I'd like
to unburden,
but not to regret, and not
undetermine,
for sin is most sweet
when wet
on the breath,
still fresh on the tongue,
still strong in
the lungs . . ."

then pausing
a moment to sip
a bit more, she
slumped, mum
as a nun,
rolled up for the night
in the sacrosanct,
wine-sticky
hug
of a fuzzy-
napped, plenteous,
possum-
white rug.

Memoirs

A story,
a story (a
rhapsode is
horny),
a drama,
a drama
(a sighing slips
from her),
a thief on
the job,
the rust-trunk
of memory (the
rhapsode says
mammaries)
to borrow or rob;
an urge to
divulge (a surge to
unbulge)
a lament,
a foment,
a soupçon and pinch-
bit (*I*
never . . .) of succulent
torment (*I always,*
I ever),
a fathomed
compendium
of first
person rations
(a grand
mastication)

deemed prurient,
and pertinent,
and food for
the nation.

O Sorrow, O Bother

O Sorrow, O Bother, a lover
who loved her
has grown weary of her,
has sloughed her and snubbed her
and washed his hands
of her,
so she's sticking a pin, again and again
in a fiendish maneuver,
a re-voodoo do-over,
like a perfected,
known sin
into an intricate doll,
its red paper, rather small
heart
and all of its parts, its toes
and its kidneys,
its spleen and its pinkies,
the knees and the jigglies; she's sticking
and sticking
and all the while thinking
and smiling while thinking
of how much it must hurt him
to be pricked by her pin,
to be hung by his thumbs
in the spin of her brain; thinking
and thinking with unended
unblinking, unbended
immersion,
of the lover
who loved her,
and grew weary
of her.

Loneliness

Envy will empty
your wallet,
embarrassment pin-nip your skin,
grief take a steel ball-
peen hammer
to your most brittle
ribbings, but this
will nickel-
and-dime you to
death. Even
beauty, quietly
carrying her candle
into a room
looks first for a mirror;
even worship with her stiff
housemaid's knee
will index and face-paint
the gods.
The arrogant inmate
alone in his flesh
strokes at his pillow,
keeps the rare,
seeded sweet for his mouse,
while the eremite high
on his pillar
pretties his eyebrows, plucks
at his scabs,
begs of the sundown
to hurry
the moon.

Mono No Aware

Less than tristesse,
but more

than a sufferably bored
ennui;

not as loud or
as proud as

a cheap
melancholy;

not so boozy
(a cup of rice

wine versus
tumbler

of whisky),
and not close

to as rheumy,
as gloom.

Not as dark
as the doldrums,

or as glum
as a funk, and in

there somewhere
creeps a nearly tear-

jerking bitter-
sweet housed

in the faint,
passing breath of a sensed

incompleteness.
One moment,

a fist-gripping, toe-
clenching,

cemented, remembered
connection

of flesh,
then in the span

of a sigh and a dip,
a rapid,

resistless, and
vividly

limbless,
extinction in mist.

Mockingbird

No other song
                    or swoop (part
                quiver, part swivel and
                    plash) with
        tour de force
stray the course note
            liquefactions
    (its new,
bawdy air an
        aria hangs in) en-
thralls,
            trills, loops, soars,
                    startles, out-warbles,
out-brawns, more
            juicily,
                lifts up
the dawn, outlaws from
                        sackcloth, the cool
        sloth of bed sheets,
                        from pillows
                and silks
                and blue-quilted, feminine
bolsters, fusses
            of coverlets;
                        nips as the switch
    of a juvenile willow, fuzz
                of a nettle, to
            window and window
                        and window and ever
                toward egress, to
                flurry, pollen
        and petal shed,

                        to wet street
and wet pavement,
                all sentiment intemperate,
    all sentience
                ephemeral.

Sex Odalisque

Pity the still of the sitter's
routine, recumbently stuck in her dull rapture rut,
par for the course, and no
worse for the wear. What static, vacuous labor
it takes, to stretch out a couch, to keep a look put,
the de facto embargo

on rising or sighing, not to fritter
an itch, not straighten a slouch or tuck in a foot
but to remain so ably, so
complacently lush, contained and unstirred
attained and untouched.

Sex Rubenesque

Unleash the excess!
Bring me cleavage and rumpage,
one heftable breast, then another,
a buttock untrussed
and rhapsodic for humpage.
Begin the maneuvers,

purge girdles and covers; undress
all strumpets of frumpages
that revolt a fat lover. Release the noblesse,
the cankles and haunch, trot out the lumpage—
Deliver the flesh!

From the Grandiloquent Dictionary

Tragematopolist

Ah, my bon bon mama, put up your stuff,
your nuts and nougats, your marshmallow fluffs;
show me the gum drops, the Zotz and Pop Rocks,
the wax lips, the whips, your heart-red Red Hots.

Rhyparographer

Her canvas: *American Vanitas,*
morbid enough, and sufficiently crass
to repel a leper, shock all cynics,
appal psychotics, and charm the critics.

Nellipot

Too sad a soot he tracked along his road,
too flat and dragged his foot, too hammer-toed,
too bereft of sidecar or plush chauffeur
to be shod with a misnomered loafer.

Whither the Lamplight,

huggermuggery fan-dance,
                              or so ask
the poets, and, homage aside, asks I.

Whither the blackcloth, the blindfold, blind eye,
whispered apocrypha, tumbrel-trod risk,

and whence the appeal of such minds areel,
such minds as ours, our internal curtsies

and barnstorms at half-light, our small, hearty
awes, our deadman's hand tells. Whither the fell

of the rotted wheel-rut, the shanghaied, old
nebulae, dirty old snowballs, whence urge

of the skull-lip atremble, the largesse
from forfeit, dodgier moon, whence scald, scald

of words as they fall, their vein-purr, myrrh-stain:
Niagara, Niagara, O roar again!

The Old Woman Gets Drunk with the Moon

The moon is rising everywhere;
The moon's my favorite easy chair,
My tin pot-top, my green plum tree,
My brassy buttoned cavalry
Tap-dancing up a crystal stair.

O watch them pitch and take the air!
Like shoo fly pies and signal flares,
Like clotted cream and bumblebees,
The moons are rising.

How hits-the-spot, how debonair,
What swooned balloons of savoir faire,
What purr of rain-blurred bright marquees
That linger late, that wait for me,
Who'll someday rest my cold bones there
In moons that rise up everywhere.

Boys of L.A.

The blossom mouths of the boys of L.A.
at the torn light, at the finish of day,
with their Gaulois lips, with their coddled scars
in the quiet of large, gossamer cars,
with a toyed pose, with a grandeured dismay

born of allure of a well-oiled soiree
fawn a lost grace, yawn a more Roman way,
speak brutal lingoes of delicate bars
of blossom mouthed boys.

The tall palms stutter and stall mid-sashay,
refusing pomp, apostatizing sway
under the stare of clear, cognizant stars,
the sputter and fizz of joy-hissing stars,
that circus the night, the raucous cachet
of the blossom mouths of boys of L.A.

The Voluminous Diva

The voluminous diva David loved,
a temptress of flesh and comely cream puff
measured in meters and athletically stuffed

into a bustier unwisely sized *small,*
ahead a cortege down a tall mirrored hall,
down the length and the width of the tall mirrors saw

drawn taut in dark satin, lit from above,
a breaching of seams in the south region of
a diva not trussed, or buttressed, enough.

Having Discovered a Windfall by the Side of the Road, the Cautious Miser Is Visited by the Angel of Profligacy

Our most perfect machine.
    See it wink in the dirt. See it flirt.

How it warms in the hand.
    See it rubbed in the glove. See it shine.

See it deepen and gleam. *How it bursts.*
    No coin is an island;

no tender unclean.
    How it sweetens the feast of the beast of the heart.

How the heart is a clasp, is a reasoned last stand.
    Let us splurge on its worth, let us dine.

Let it simmer and burn, let us thirst.
    Let us fill if you will. Let it flash, let it spend.

Let it tend like a fire-coal dark in the pocket,
    like a radiant coffer.
                Unlock it, unlock it!

The Roshi in the Mirror

To begin
with a not yet
lost
thought:

If you said you
were *I,*
you
would be telling
a lie.

And if I said I,
as if I were speaking
of *me,*
then I
would be
someone,
most likely not you
(that toeless
and eyeless
and tongueless
old

shoe),
trying
as hard
as I could
and as far as
I should
(like
a fleetingest,
speechlessest,
egoless

flea) (like
the unstoppable
drip of
an impalpable
drop)
to

be what
I am and what
I am not.

Pip, Mid-Sea

Dear muddler and paddler of puddles,
dear huddler of egotist oceans,
dear floater, dear rower of mania,
your captain is calling,
a god of horizon, a lord of the maelstrom.
He's roaring and rumbling;
he has a lantern in hand;
he has a whale by the tail,
your pilot, your master.
Dear lunatic wader,
delirious thrasher, white horses saddler,
dear fop of glad madness,
take grip of your wits,
your buoy, your ballast;
come back to your helmsman;
return to your wheelman,
your whaler, your angler, your savior, your anchor.

Rescue

Sometimes it gets there
routinely,
with less of a trumpeted burst
than a tepid,
and expected,
trickle.
Sometimes it's a bowl
of cold rice
with no meat and no gravy,
a glass of flat water,
no lime and no ice.
Sometimes a country that doesn't
love life
forgets the confetti
but still sends a cab;
sometimes the boys at the lab
ship the vaccine and pocket
the profit,
lick their fingertips
clean.
Once in a lifetime
a chorus of persons
courageous
will dogsled Alaska
or tunnel through stone
with a great oom pah pah,
but mostly it's someone
who's weary and common
slogging dumb mud
to a middling hurrah.

Brass Knuckles

If they could speak, they would
mumble;

they would stumble
and stammer like

Demosthenes' pebbles,
in an attempt to spit

out, between grout
and loose gneiss, *How*

'bout those Mets, or
Give us a kiss.

On nights when they're twitchy,
they might reach for a shot

of the warm, raw, amber-
lit solace

of unblended whisky,
while on days when

they're dizzy
with business, they hum.

No one reveres them
and they prefer no

one does; would have
their existence

iconoclastic and
stolidly

lyric,
swaddled in rag cloth

or plastic or burlap
or any loose fabric

resigned
to abuse, kept within

reach in the clancular
backs of rolltop desk drawers,

or tossed like white-
hot potatoes

down crepuscular
stairs

of irregular cellars.

From the Grandiloquent Dictionary

Famulus

Saw me in half, suspend or submerge me,
light me on fire and swallow the key;
I'm your one sure ruse, no smoke, no mirrors,
no flinch of fear or visible wires.

Hophound

Poor Dan is in a droop, muddled with dope
he's dropped and skin-popped and snorted and smoked,
pie- and glass-eyed, coked up without question,
happy past any best-laid redemption.

Venusaphobia

Ever since fabled *Madam I'm Adam,*
our stunned cerebellums have stammered dumb,
our backbones and bowels, our ludicrous knees
flinched and quivered like a young Sweet Gum tree.

Zen Heaven

No melon, no lemon, no scone, no crumb,
no tuns of gin or barrels of bourbon,
no chocolate chiffon, no filet mignon.

No bumped shins, no bunions, no rain-ached bones,
no lesions or abrasions, no spasms,
nothing swollen, fallen, rotten, or numb.

No courtesans or virgins, no woman
or man. No estrogen, progesterone,
not one lone hormone to scorn or condone.

No vision, no mission, no chosen son,
no inaction or action, no outcome
of passion, no function, done or undone.

No lesson at the end, no dead dial tone.
No one in the tomb, no tomb, no tombstone.

Notes

"From the Grandiloquent Dictionary": To read definitions of these, and other fabulous words, see *Grandiloquent Dictionary* at www.islandnet.com/~egbird/dict/dict.htm.

—*Rhyparographer: American Vanitas* is a work by Merry Fuhrer.

"Whither the Lamplight,": This title is a line from a poem by Mark Bibbins.

Hailey Leithauser's work has appeared widely for over a decade in the *Antioch Review*, the *Gettysburg Review*, *Pleiades*, *Poetry*, the *Southwest Review*, in the *Best American Poetry* and *Best New Poets* anthologies, and on *Poetry Daily* and *Verse Daily*. She is a winner of the Discovery/*The Nation* Award, the Elizabeth Matchett Stover Award, the *River Styx* International Poetry Award, and a recipient of an independent artists grant from the Maryland State Arts Council. Her first book, *Swoop*, received the Emily Dickinson First Book Award from the Poetry Foundation. She lives in the Maryland suburbs of Washington, DC.

Book design by Connie Kuhnz. Composition by BookMobile Design and Digital Publisher Services, Minneapolis, Minnesota. Manufactured by Versa Press on acid-free 30 percent postconsumer wastepaper.